On each page of this word book is a lively, colorful scene. Lots of things are happening in each picture, to draw the child's attention and stimulate his or her interest and imagination. Some scenes will be familiar ones; some will be more unusual. All have been chosen to intrigue and interest, and to prompt thoughts and questions.

Picked out around the busy scenes are single items, all labeled so that the child can look, point out, identify and say the words out loud. Later, he or she will be able to read the words. The 300 words have been carefully chosen to provide a mixture of familiar and new words— and there is a useful alphabetical word list at the back of the book.

Copyright © MCMLXXXIII by World International Publishing Limited
All rights reserved throughout the world.
Published 1985 by Derrydale Books.
Distributed by Crown Publishers, Inc.
Printed in Belgium.
ISBN 0 517 479982.

hgfedcba

a child's first book of

words

words by Brenda Apsley

pictures by Peter Broadbent

DERRYDALE BOOKS
New York

house

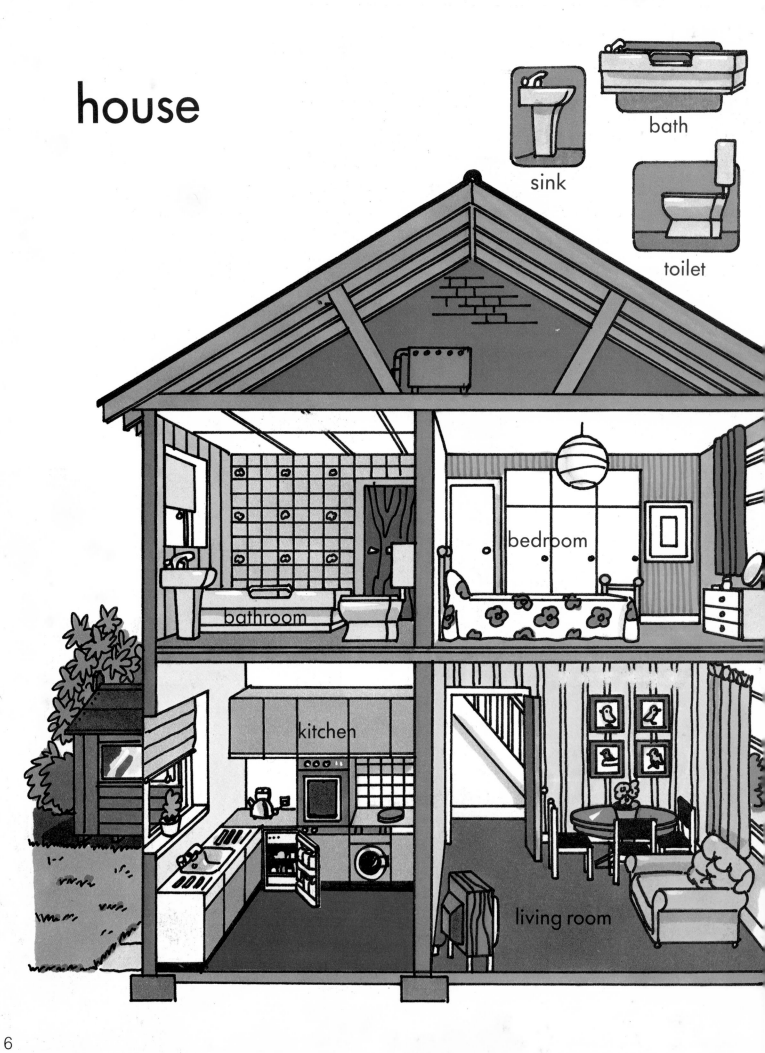

sink

bath

toilet

bedroom

bathroom

kitchen

living room

6

closet

drawers

television

sofa

bed

chair

carpet

table

oven

kettle

washing machine

refrigerator

door

window

garden

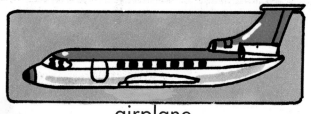
airplane

pilot

luggage

flight attendant

windsock

control tower

baggage cart

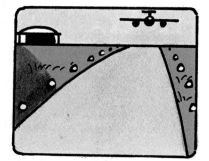
runway

landing lights

helicopter

check-in desk

hangar

fuel truck

airport

farm

barn

sheep

pond

farmer

tractor

hays

field

lambs

calf

geese

pig

horse

hens

plow

goat

sheep dog

donkey

cow

farmhouse

orchard

swing

racing car

robot

doll house

puppet

marbles

doll

rocking horse

train

building blocks

soldiers

ball

castle

boat

typewriter

teddy bear

toy shop

globe

ink

blackboard

ruler

thumb tacks

chalk

books

map

paints

brushes

pencils

paper

calendar

desk

teacher

pen

scissors

school

city

bus stop

road sign

car

police car

factory

traffic lights

shop

movie theater

crosswalk

16

truck

house

church

office building

policeman

taxi

apartments

17

tugboat

hovercraft

buoy

crane

warehouse

barge

net

lighthou

oil tanke

harbor

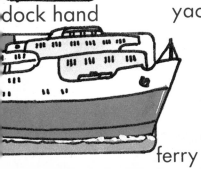
dock hand

yacht

fishing boat

anchor

ferry

life
preserver

sailor

fisherman

19

nurse

bed

chart

thermometer

doctor

x-ray

crutches

cast

bandage

wheelchair

slippers

nightgown

dressing gown

pajamas

orderly

ambulance

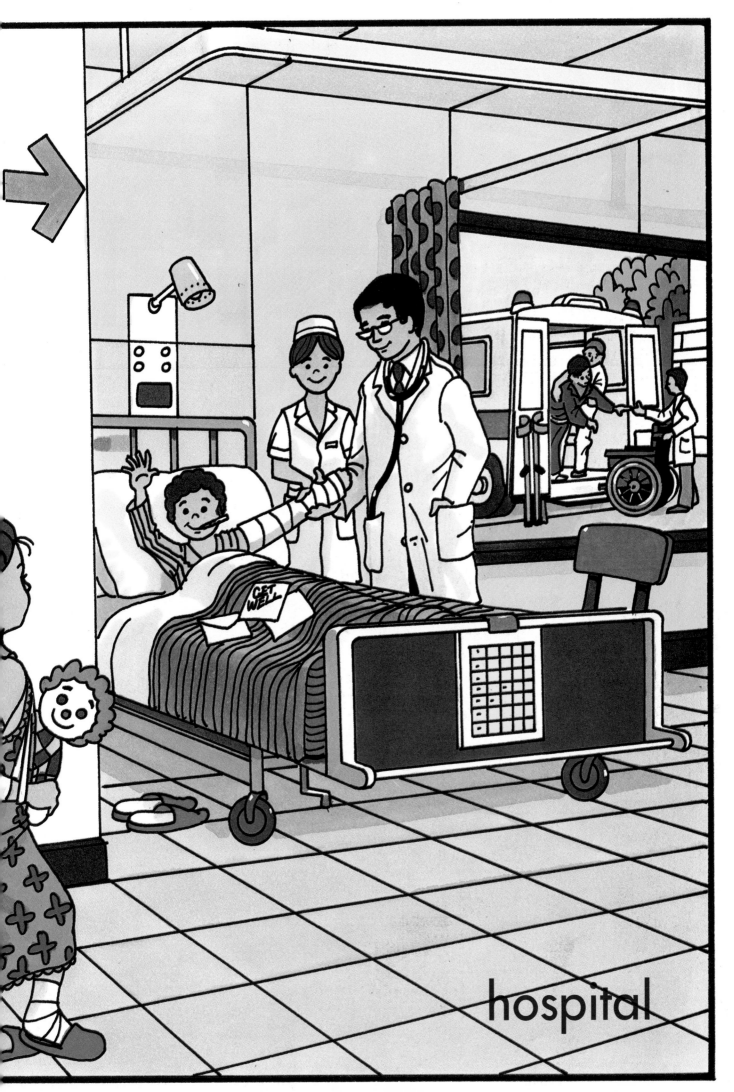

hospital

ZOO

ostrich

snake

elephant

panda

parrot

porcupine

monkey

hippopotamus

dolphin

lion

tiger

kangaroo

zebra

penguin

camel

bear

koala

giraffe

fountain

statue

bench

flower bed

swing

duck

park

merry-go-round

jungle gym

slide

tree

pond

fence

see-saw

25

railway station

train

driver

guard

engi

ticket collector

ticket office

bus station

bus

driver

conductor

passengers

line

destination board

- - - - - No.12
- - - No.14

dress

t-shirt

shorts

skirt

blouse

jeans

sandals

shoes

boots

hat

gloves

cap

socks

undershirt

coat

jacket

track suit

shirt

28

clothes

circus

ring master

acrobat

trapeze

sea lion

bear

bareback rider

clown

monkey

elephant

dog

juggler

horse 31

fire station

fire engine

fireman

alarm bell

water

axe

helmet

ladder

smoke

seaside

star fish

crab

sun

sand

sea

mask

seaweed

bucket

spade

sailboat

34

gull

seashells

flippers

flag

swimsuit

umbrella

deck chair

pebbles

35

building site

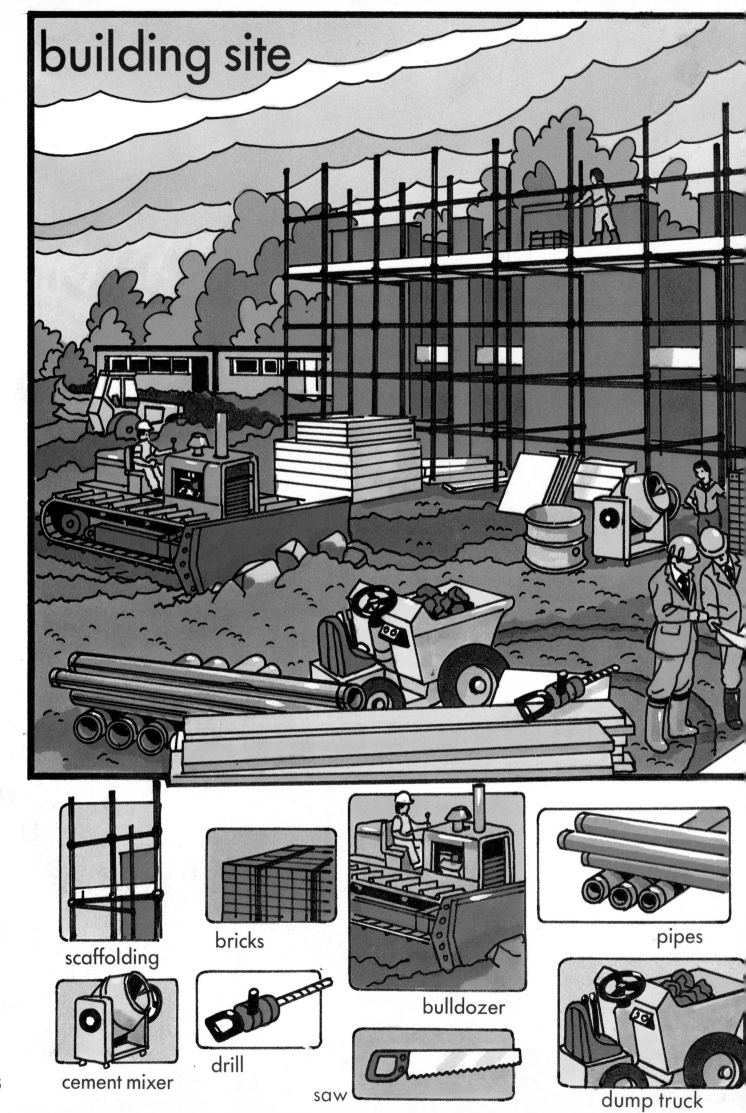

scaffolding

bricks

bulldozer

pipes

cement mixer

drill

saw

dump truck

36

tractor

spade

water

crane

wood

hammer

wheelbarrow

37

food

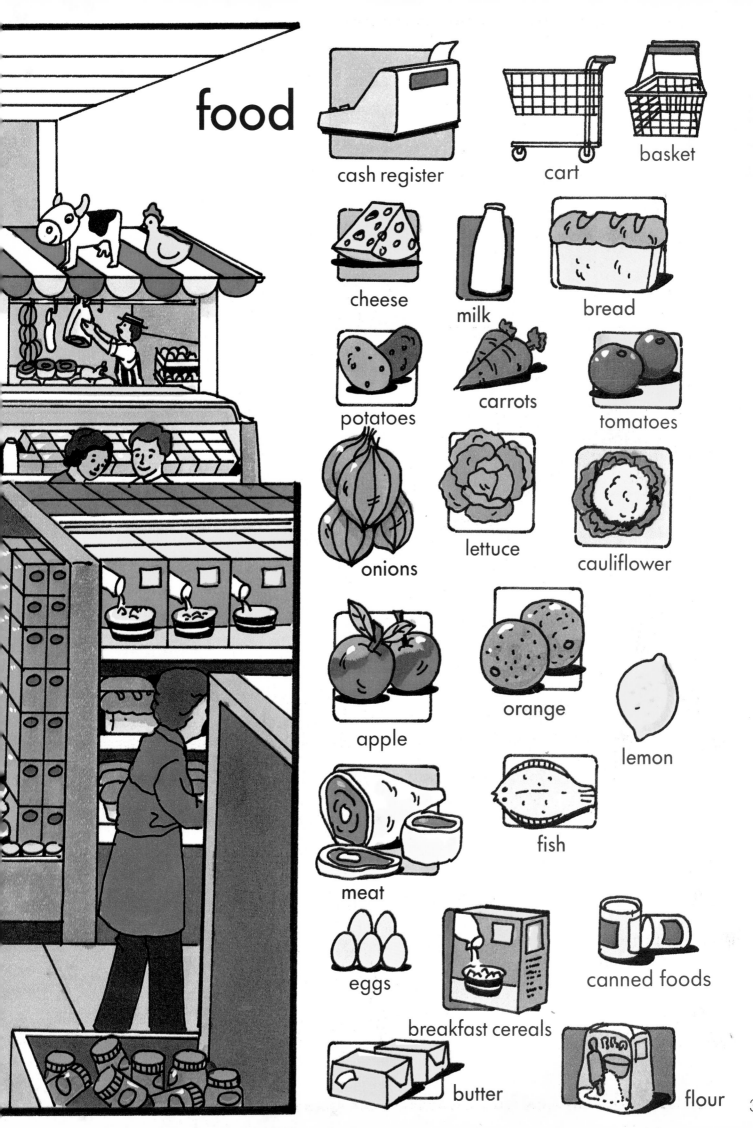

cash register

cart

basket

cheese

milk

bread

potatoes

carrots

tomatoes

onions

lettuce

cauliflower

apple

orange

lemon

meat

fish

eggs

breakfast cereals

canned foods

butter

flour

pet shop

dog

cat

puppy

kitten

goldfish

mouse

leash

hamster

rabbit

parrot

brush

parakeet

food bowl

turtle

cage

motorcycle

air pump

gas pump

tow truck

battery

oil

gas truck

truck

garage

tires

car

shop

mechanic

engine

43

word list

acrobat
airplane
airport
air pump
alarm bell
ambulance
anchor
apartments
apple
axe

boat
book
boot
bread
breakfast cereal
brick
brush
bucket
building blocks
building site
bulldozer
buoy
bus
bus station
bus stop
butter

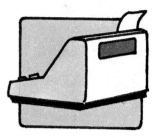

cash register
cast
castle
cat
cauliflower
cement mixer
chair
chalk
chart
check-in desk
cheese
church
circus
city
closet
clothes
clown

baggage cart
ball
bandage
bareback rider
barge
barn
basket
bath
bathroom
battery
bear
bed
bedroom
bench
blackboard
blouse

cage
calendar
calf
camel
canned foods
cap
car
carpet
cart
carrot

coat
conductor
control tower
cow
crab
crane
crosswalk
crutches

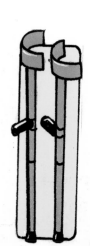

44

deck chair
desk
destination board
dock hand
doctor

dog
doll
doll house
dolphin
donkey
door
drawers

factory
farm
farmer
farm house
fence
ferry
field
fire engine
fireman
fire station
fish

fisherman
fishing boat
flag
flight attendant
flippers
flour
flower bed
food
food bowl
fountain
fuel truck

globe
glove
goat
goldfish
guard
gull

hammer
hamster
hangar
harbor
hat
haystack
helicopter
helmet
hen
hippo
horse
hospital
house
hovercraft

dress
dressing gown
drill
driver
duck
dump truck

egg
elephant
engine

garage
garden
gas pump
gas truck
geese
giraffe

ink

jacket
jeans
juggler
jungle gym

kangaroo
kettle
kitchen
kitten
koala

45

ladder
lamb
landing light
leash
lemon
lettuce
life preserver
lighthouse
line
lion
living room
luggage

map
marbles
mask
meat
mechanic
merry-go-round
milk
monkey
motorcycle
mouse
movie
    theater

net
nightgown
nurse

office building
oil
oil tanker
onion
orange
orchard
orderly
ostrich
oven

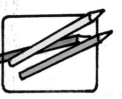

paint
pajamas
panda
paper
parakeet
park
parrot
passenger
pebble
pen
pencil
penguin
pet shop
pig
pilot
pipe
plow
police car
policeman

pond
porcupine
potatoes
puppet
puppy

rabbit
racing car
railway station
refrigerator
ring master
road sign
robot
rocking horse
ruler
runway

sailboat
sailor
sand
sandals
saw
scaffolding
school
scissors
sea